WHAT BOOKS PRESS

AN IMPRINT OF

THE GLASS TABLE

COLLECTIVE

LOS ANGELES

ALSO BY LYNNE THOMPSON

Beg No Pardon
Through A Window
We Arrive By Accumulation

START WITH A SMALL GUITAR

POEMS

LYNNE THOMPSON

WHAT
BOOKS
PRESS

LOS ANGELES

Poems in this collection appeared in their present and earlier versions in the following publications: "The Long Look" in *Affilia*; "Note Left on the Bedpost for My Ordinary Icarus" and "Start with a Small Guitar" in *Aperçus Quarterly*; "The Long Look," Finalist, 2007 Lois Cranston Memorial Poetry Prize, in *Calyx*; "Gyre" and "Zuma Beach, 1968" in *Connotations Press*; "More Than a Rhythm Section," in *Dogwood*; "Time & Want" in *Fox Chase Review*; "—Last Night, I Dreamed I Was Frida Kahlo—" in *In Posse Review*; "Monarch" in *Jet Fuel Review*; "Delusion, *an urban romance*" in *Pedestal*; "Optimist's Requiem" and "The New Eroticism" in *Poemeleon*; "Metronome, *lately adagio*," "Modern Sonnet of Augury," and "Wishbone" in *Pool;* "Empathy" and "The Day I Left You" in *Tab, The Journal of Poetry & Poetics;* "Shall" in *Zócalo Public Square*.

Special thanks and appreciation to Dorothy Barresi, Karen Kevorkian, Candace Pearson, and David St. John. This collection exists because they insisted upon it.

Publisher's Cataloging-In-Publication Data
Thompson, Lynne, 1951-
  Start with a small guitar : poems / Lynne Thompson.
    p. ; cm.
  ISBN: 978-0-9889248-3-3
  1. Love--Poetry. 2. American poetry--21st century. 3. Experimental poetry, American. I. Title.

PS3620.H6836 S73 2013
811/.6

What Books Press
10401 Venice Boulevard, no. 437
Los Angeles, California 90034

WHATBOOKSPRESS.COM

Cover art: Gronk, *Untitled*, 2012
Book design by Ashlee Goodwin, Fleuron Press

START WITH A SMALL GUITAR

CONTENTS

The Long Look   11

Zuma Beach, 1968—   13

Monarch   14

—Last Night, I Dreamed I Was Frida Kahlo—   15

Afterburn   16

To Love In This World, Ask   17

Little Song of Alcove   18

Modern Sonnet of Augury   19

Note Left on the Bedpost for My Ordinary Icarus   20

You Speak to Me of Glitter,   21

Duel   22

The New Eroticism   23

Midnight, *or later,*   24

. . . But Anyway, I Am a Woman . . .   25

Gyre   27

Shall   28

Nature Boy's   29

Wishbone   30

More Than a Rhythm Section,   31

Amber. Shadow. Thorn.   33

Empathy   35

Ars Poetica, *ruthless*   36

Laceum   37

Ars Poetica, *prayer*   38

The Sweet Blind   39

Sea   40

Time & Want   42

The Day I Left You   43

Last Elegy for the Red Dress   44

Metronome, *lately adagio*   45

Optimist's Requiem   46

Start with a Small Guitar   47

A Book of Questions in the End   48

Delusion, *an urban romance*   50

Precipice   51

This is the way of love and music: it plays like a god and
then is done.

Roxanne Beth Johnson
Blues for Almost Forgotten Music

THE LONG LOOK

—this boy I am remembering
      put his eyes on me—

he stepped out of his body
and let it pool around his ankles
      like a lagoon—

      He put his eyes on me

and they were shameless—

less rapacious than cling
         and shadow

and I must have looked like an icon
or a victim:

      arms, waist, shoulders
and their blades, butt and kneecaps
all of me   an improbable bargain

Still, he didn't take his eyes away—

just let them unbend   then open

    like envelopes

        while he inhaled,

looked at my wrists and heels and
any other part of my anatomy
he had not yet oppressed—

Darkly, my flesh turned

and my skin, wanting, spoke:

            don't   please

but he wasn't finished—

ZUMA BEACH, 1968—

one year past the Summer of Love, my yellow Mustang designed for more
than the Sunset Strip, we drove past Santa Monica's pier, the Colony, and our
curfew. We floored it, then parked by the moon and the grunion. We brought
a flask of Mt. Gay rum but it wasn't enough. I can't remember the name of my
make me wanna shout or whether it was him or the automatic gear that ripped
through my scanties. What I remember was the drifter—his eyes as grave as
unnamed planets, his breath piercing the fog outside our fogged-up windshield;
his mouth, greedy and toothless, as he drooled for what we all want: to grapple
with flesh. Even now, I think I hear his laugh—raucous and raw—like a
raven's.

MONARCH

He whispered it a few times—naughty—
and it sounded childlike (as if I was still
a child) and sensual until I remembered:
sensual and childlike are forbidden to lie
in such close juxtaposition though I do not
recall who said so. Who was it, after all,

who proclaimed children are innocents when
we have many reasons to know they are not?
Why just today, I saw a shy girl pull a butterfly
from its flight, detach each of its wings & hold
each gossamer bit, whole—with such ferocious
tenderness—between her willing ruby lips.

—LAST NIGHT, I DREAMED
I WAS FRIDA KAHLO—

star-tips and tight earth,
beaver, pond, blue veronica.
I wasn't Frida but I was
just as unfathomable
being roots & thistle & blood,
bulb of green earth, womb
of some wingéd web-weaver,
deep lover, quite still, still
stone. In morning's indigo,
in the steam and sun of it all,
I was supplicant before oceans,
apatite, ideas and lantern-
light, unhooked and needle-
fine, copper-red, a cosmos—

AFTERBURN

Maybe I had to love him when he told me he and his boys

hijacked summer afternoons and laid—spread-eagle—

on the local airstrip, waiting for the two-seaters to rev up

and tip their wings skyward then soar—after-burn burning

the boys' cheeks, filth of the bird's exhaust flooding their lungs.

That's what I drank when he kissed me and when he kissed me,

I recall, is when I turned eager daredevil & barn-storming fool.

TO LOVE IN THIS WORLD, ASK

what draws the body in?

The passionate restraint—
the progress of a drawn line

disappearing—a striving for
nuance to frame the tango?

LITTLE SONG OF ALCOVE

Velocity of a child's laugh
or bantamweight like a leaf

just as the poets describe—
yes. Yes. It was like that.

All about us, those we duped.
No one saw because

our shadows were just mere
dazzle across the landscape

and spells and delight last only
so long and then the violence

of remembering takes hold.
It was that way. Chisel of *can't*

keep: his mouth, new, on mine—
both of us unexceptional fools.

MODERN SONNET OF AUGURY

It must be that my sleeping is sleeping, stealing dreams. In a Time-Before-Fathom was cockle-shell, wind chime. In Nodding was feather—walnuts, halves sewn shut—one simple stone. Neither storm-wrecked nor melancholy was and dreaming did not know mauve as blush. Ignominy grew no tendrils around an urgency free of its clock. In star-shine, loath to give up its secrets, was no pride. Until invention, all was at rest. Invention, with its needles and promise: revenge. Sleeping shifted. Ladder-like, sea-grass climbed sea-grass, broke every surface. Rain tasted the sour of itself. Stopped: song of two parrots. Lure of causeways: stopped. Ditto the shovel and cross leaving only two questions: love and love...

...or, there's a lake, and in the middle of (this isn't a dream) the lake, there is something pretending (as you and I are pretending) to be a boat with glass riggings. In the mainsail, riff of blues becoming. The boat has (or hasn't had) passengers save one (me? you?) who holds the paddle and the paddle is level with the water (walk on) and the water is still (deep running) and the water gives in to its temperature although nothing is Fahrenheit only (*sooner or later it all comes down to faith*) on a lake in the middle of...

NOTE LEFT ON THE BEDPOST
FOR MY ORDINARY ICARUS

From more than my balcony,
you leap—patchouli in air,
hymn like a wheel, a fiction
turned hurricane on an atoll.

You are ever-young, hair
slicked from your temples.
You are color and no color
and a pyre and

more harming than harmed.
I'll be sleeping when you come
fish-bait, skim-over-sheer-water.
Leave the letter you promised,

precious between the blue of
its syllables, brine in its crease.
Place its weight on my temple,
my strange, quicksilver birdie.

YOU SPEAK TO ME OF GLITTER,

and I to you, of a white goat,
a love of highlands, strangeness,
an appetite for clean, clear spaces.
You don't speak of what matters.

Of my love of highlands, strangeness,
you thrust out your tongue in distress.
You won't speak of what matters, of
what I want: to be keen-eyed, knowing.

You thrust out your tongue in distress
at the cardinal's wing I bring you,
at my keen eye & dazzled knowing
there is no cure for mournful singing…

Look at the cardinal's wing I bring you
and my appetite for clean, clear spaces.
Where's the cure for mournful singing
when I speak to you of the white goat?

DUEL

When he speaks,
I hear *tripwire*.

When I shift,
he sees *malfeasance*.

Breakfast is frogs
and a bitter cup.

Lovering has highs
when it isn't baroque.

Months honeycomb.
Years boil my legs as

wry as a mermaid's.
His face is lovely

as a stanza—
as a starter's gun;

my mouth
is upside down, inside.

THE NEW EROTICISM

Because the 21st century has ditched
that old-school road to romance,
you have found a new way to seduce me.
Rather than stroke the honey-spot
where my neck succumbs
to a shoulder that could wonder you,
you stroke keys on some small black widget
held in your palm
until your want of me
glows green on the screen,
takes several minutes to reach me
with its *ChiGong* tune and then,
with no one near me knowing why,
causes my cheeks to redden.
Gone the parchment papers
with love sop writ in peacock blue.
Gone the 2 A.M. whispers
under cover of an inexhaustible dark,
only a telephone wire between us.
And because the time is now
and we can never go back
and because I want you
to inhale deeply, *deeply*, then whistle,
I press fingers to my own widget's keys:
enter   enter   enter

MIDNIGHT, *OR LATER,*

in the small hours, I sleep
without sleeping.
Prone, I am wilderness,

recall and amnesia.
He comes dressed in his costume,
cradles my mask in his hands...

... BUT ANYWAY, I AM A WOMAN ...

....he knows that.
Knows it the same way he knows
no matter how hard he tries
to define himself as spark plug or whiskey neat,
I will come back
in the late night
(as I always do, lately)
to prove myself more than other-worldly,
to prove that whether he tosses
you can't hold me or cow patties in my path,
I will grind all of it
into the mute earth that has birthed him.
Knowing doesn't make it any better;
doesn't stop the veins in his body
from madly twisting the way a hundred spiders
might twist upon themselves
in a mirrored, haunted house.
He knows about *haunted*,
about the axis in constant rotation,
the inconvenience.
No matter how hard he tries,
the vision of my mouth and aspect remains,
my mourning and my survival...

———

...my mourning and my survival,
the vision of my mouth and aspect remains.
No matter how hard I try—
despite the inconvenience,
the axis in constant rotation,
I know about *haunted*
as in mirrored, haunted houses
twisting upon themselves, madly twisting,
the way a hundred spiders might.
The veins in my body knowing
doesn't make it any better.
Into the mute earth that has birthed me,
I grind all of it;
put *you can't hold me* and cow patties in the path
wherever he tosses himself,
to prove myself more than other-worldly
(always and lately)
in the late night
when I come back
to define him as spark plug or whiskey neat
no matter how hard he tries.
It's that way.
I know that...

GYRE

All his volleyball of language

(the spiraling outward
of its giddy-up and

wordplay)
can't hold a candle

to his tongue
in my earbox,

his hand deeply into
my pocket of thighs

even when mute me—
blank page—disappears

into candle-light   beneath
     less than   until—

                    *

He failed, of course,
to take
what should be
taken daily;

almost took me,
me of the trembling breast,
one small fist gripped
around a homicidal pen.

SHALL

—there is an under the table under the table and under that the quick
narrow   whirling   and beneath that stars shining like feldspar
liking the sound of their life as feldspar   Farther below
someone speaks in a language mislaid while
beneath that
sixteen bay horses bray   but unlike the wind
they wind round and around a corral like prisoners of Zen
with keys to an incredible door
or an unincredible door   nearby
and we who are underneath go through
and come out where there is no next to
where anemones and coral and cobalt's blue as Chet Baker
but only for moments because tuning   always tuning   are bassoons
flutes   an orchestra that can't harmonize the rattling and quaking and mizzle
misting for days to avoid all that decrees   even in this flickering *here*
in these little pieces   *thou shall not—*

NATURE BOY'S

a wire bird. Wiry bird.

    Bead.
    Bangle.
    Boswain

on a slow boat to China,
        come hither. Heather

on the hill. Hillock. Shiver me
timberland, a wolf's head,

    worry.
    Wrong.
    Song

like leaf shimmer, worm glow.

Positively not, Spot. How he runs…

WISHBONE

The problems I have are few
at this time:

      an absurd arithmetic
      of desire—
      a certain political
      absence.

These storms present
without solution:
all the lipstick in the world—
all the choirs and buttressing
of angels atop cathedrals—oh,
how easily women are fooled.

All I have is a drawer
of fetching charms.
Does anyone know
why I keep them:
satinwood, nails,
one camisole and its metal,
phylactery, this mousetrap?

MORE THAN A RHYTHM SECTION,

I want a band.

I want a band
that low-tones
downtown
in smoky bars.

I want a band
that highbrows
with hot cats
in the uptown—
there is a rose
in Spanish Harlem—
of lamp-lit lofts.

I want
but they say
money's tight
and *what about*
a baby and *you*
can't have it all.

But I want rests & scales
and a tenor voice to
sing softly to me
and musicians who sit
where woodwinds
and brass sit and when
the best is yet to come

I want my man
to tuba me,
trombone me
and flare my bells,
to oboe and O baby
love me `til I swing low
who will buy
this wonderful feelin'?

AMBER. SHADOW. THORN.

She made an offhand promise to no one in particular:
she would only love men who were leaving for war—

whether they had been called upon by the legislators
or whether they had taken the call upon themselves,

whether they came from homes where their mothers
needed them to mend garden tiles or tile the eaves,

whether they were offspring of the fare-thee-wells or
whether they looked to land beyond a corner office.

If they were looking good in their brass button fantasies
or even if an ill-fitting uniform fit their bodies poorly,

she would love them. Unsure of her plan or provocation,
she would love them on afternoons the color of napalm.

She would love them before their skins reeked of a scorch
yet to be smelled, that stink that tattoos us all through time.

She would pour two fingers of bourbon while she loved them,
then daub it across her breasts and belly for their amusement.

She would love them in the bed that had been her father's—
a man who foiled his summons to war and was never the same

but she didn't love them for this reason alone and the ways these
men loved her was a talisman in the smoke over the blood-fields.

With no expectation of a dispatch or other aide-mémoire that
she'd ever been loved, she was a Jesus thorn, festering for them.

She tried, once, to love a man who was committed to nothing;
he smelled of alluvium and excuses and, despised, was sent away.

Chastely, she loved the gone-to-war when her body's talent no
longer could. One of them came home—with scored flesh and

amputation—to find her. He found an empty house, amber liquor
in vials, one torn mattress, shadow and want stippling the cool air.

EMPATHY

I don't care what you do. Find some-
one rounder or anyone who smells like
what you remember of persimmon.

Remember last summer? Violence was
only a rehearsal and we were so much
older, more fruitful. I don't care again.

There's going to be another intifada.
There's going to be a wind-up and we'll
be sitting in an Olvera Street café, eating

frijoles and what's left of our young.
Please don't pretend you don't
remember this or any other lie—

I saw you. I saw a winter moth succumb,
clutched between your nervy thumbs.
I saw you kill it with your dirty spoon.

ARS POETICA, *RUTHLESS*

Like every woman duped by prayer,
our patter comes in sets of three:
believing, unrelated, naked. No one
is upright. No one moves noiselessly.
Language is a porcupine; beggar bones
slighting flesh; filaments   kissing.

LACEUM

Whenever he thinks of me (he *will*), he will
think of me walking away, my body turned
against another weariness, my hips inked with
roses and he'll be convinced he can smell them,
each petal wafting its singular fragrant particular,
its own design, and he will believe that when
he saw me last, I was clothed in only blue lace,
blue as blue as the harbor at Toulon, pale blue,
forget-me-blue, blueberry, blue of the high-stepping
Prussians, of ice, of hard boys, the politics of scratch,
Egyptian blue ground from silica, copper and lime,
the indigo described by Pliny the Elder, the blue
of the cloak of Christ in the Hagia Sophia,
in the pottery at Delft or Van Gogh's *Starry Night*.
And when he recalls the lace (from the vulgar
Latin: *laceum*)—linen or silk, purl-knitted table-
cloth or doily for wounded flesh—he will recall
I was adorned with ribbons colored pink, *gulabi*,
cherry blossom, *rosa*, flamingo and Amazon dolphin.
Also our sorrow: I never stopped or turned around.

ARS POETICA, *PRAYER*

Under a subatomic swoop of shale
a lilac want chair,
sometimes a picnic of intention
or small, heedless choices.
Words are crippled moons here—
belong to the nib or the priests.
They sing of sky, then earth,
then fall, silent, into the drift.

THE SWEET BLIND

Upon my body—*perhaps*
　　the other way around?—
　　　　your four-leaf clover.

This argument—elegant—geometric—
　　assumes its own heat.
　　　　It is grander or more

reduced than desire or this chalice of
　　one day we will leave abruptly,
　　　　forget: nail of one lover's

middle toe scraping the other lover's
　　inner thoughts; their imaginations
　　　　indistinct, impossible

to separate.　Or maybe this is only a season's
　　back-story, given context; quite rare
　　　　in…shall we call it late summer?

And even as I tell you that every season
　　is rare, you, my pretty—well, let's just say
　　　　your response is as deliberate as

an artist's duplicity; subtle as the melodic *Sweet Blindness,*
　　thunderous in its rebuke of our conspiracy,
　　　　of our bodies, inflamed, and astonished—

SEA

If not imagination,
what? Science

proves you don't
see what I do

so when we agree,
whose eye is it?

My palm to yours is
a made up construct

so where's the surprise?
In a bassinet, long before

the long before, I heard
what you heard and

was glad, even when
I learned it was all

a changeable thing.
One day, your hand

will slide beneath
my most secret

secrets and *then*—
there will be the story:

our imaginations
making up the world.

TIME & WANT

You don't want to think it was you. You want to think
you were kind when you had to be; that you were more
supple in bed than a serpent when he was your shiny
apple. You want to say he mumbled when spoken to but
waxed eloquent making vulgar jokes about your mother.
You need your gal-pals to loathe him twice as much as
you do. You would love to *sweet baby love* some heart-
stopping hunk o' hunk as soon as possible, but you fear

that idea's the most improbable of all. You want to two-
step in a shower of fireflies so everyone thinks you're lovely
and always will be. You never want to get out of your bed.
Just there, you stare at ants on the march on your window
sill. Each one who isn't a queen has her task to complete,
time & again, and when she fails, she's cast from the colony.

THE DAY I LEFT YOU

there was a tremendous crash
two blocks away. No one died,

not even me. It may have been
raining but the clouds hid

everything except a mockingbird.
There were letters in the box when

I got home; I never opened them.
Later, a girl said music played

across the city; she didn't say how.
When I asked about the harmonies,

only dust replied in a language
I have never learned. The day I left,

you were draped in indecision. You
plucked a refrain from Billy Strayhorn's

Lush Life and I loved it. You said
you were hungry but never touched

your plate. I recall that it was cold;
that we were dressed only in gestures.

LAST ELEGY FOR THE RED DRESS

Good morning Red Dress—
heavy with the sweat of
Love Wants to Dance. Scented
with the hopes of Shy Man, Bold Man,
Begged-To-Take-Me-Home Man.
Still crinkly-crumply down the back
from the hanker in their hands.

Good Morning Red Dress.
`Morning chase-me, take-me shoes.
Look like you've been out on the town,
like you've been dipped and twirled,
Dizzy'd and Duke'd all night long,
like you can't hang between sweatsuits
and jeans—like you're another kinda gal.

Hello and hey there, Red Dress,
double strand of pearls, faded rose
perfume still clinging to the bodice,
the slip, the silk of the sleeve;
still molten to my hips, my breasts,
to the drum of my heart, hem
softly pleated to a permanent party.

Where've you been, Red Dress?
And why have you moved on without me?

METRONOME, *LATELY ADAGIO*

From amen to amen,
there is no grace.

Deadlines are illusory
as contrails of snow geese.

Yet, there could be *might be*

but for the muddied air
dressed in its persona: dread.

Under clay, our faltering resolve.
In the wind, gash of white noise.

OPTIMIST'S REQUIEM

Foolish fool, foolproof fool, Queen of Foolhardy Fools, fool for the long foolish haul although *Mama didn't raise no fool* isn't part of my lexicon and having a lexicon is one reason I'm such a fool. I've been fooled fifty-nine times and never fooled a single soul. I've been a fast car fool, a fool for fool's gold, an American fool and

I've volunteered everywhere that needs one. Seems I'm not interested in anything else; I think I want fool etched on my forehead. Was a time when being a fool was a slip I could have slipped out of but that was forty slips ago. Now fool is tattooed on my tattoos as I sit at the table eating beans and more beans— a farting fool, that's me.

> *I won't think of desire or anything that might turn*
> *me optimistic. It's not going to happen. I'll forget*
> *how buttons button, get the cancer and die and*
> *still be thinking   maybe   did you see that*
> *did it look like love?*

START WITH A SMALL GUITAR

although you already know: this was never a real guitar.
What you hear is the melody once resident inside you
and you know this too: it's only my silhouette you see
dancing, dancing. Step into this splendid suggestion or
flotsam. Then are those my eyes, filling, or yours?

or   start again with a small guitar

Of course, you already know: this was never a real guitar.
But here are all of my fingers longing to coax its *duende*.
What you hear is the melody once resident inside you as
it escapes, suddenly, and I am there just in time to pluck it

from the innocent air & slip it around my wrist like a cuff.
You must know this too: it's only my silhouette you see
dancing, dancing. Step into it: this splendid suggestion,
this flotsam. Then, are those my eyes, filling? Yours?

A BOOK OF QUESTIONS IN THE END

In the end,
>we are water and misery,
>misery and thin blood;

I don't remember which.

In the end,
>we put our feet into the sea
>and they return with an appetite

to jog to the end of endings:
>of dynasties,
>of coral reefs
>and outer galaxies,
>scientific postulates
>and operatic riffs;
>this indeterminable language.

In the end,
>none of our mothers are walruses
>(but their sons? all carpenters)

& they have no daughters   in the end.
>This is an illogical conclusion;
>an imperturbable enigma.

This isn't a polemic
       in the end;
       this isn't a slide rule
       or an immaculate kingdom;
       this, no funeral march
       or declaration of dependence.
       This isn't a love letter.

Was there ever real love
       at the end? That afternoon
       in Sicily or in Mexico where

finally, the champagne
       was no more sweet than
       in the back seat of our old van?

And if, in the end, I loved,
       how do the seasons know
       they must change their shirt?

The two italicized closing lines are from William O'Daly's translation of Pablo Neruda's Book of Questions, LXXII

DELUSION, *AN URBAN ROMANCE*

We live in a city ringed with false teeth.
We do not know we are living.

We are dreaming, forgetting
dreams have meaning conjoined

to tinsel and modern catastrophes.
We exhale by a sea

the color of guilt and broken jade,
the life of its whales

a slaughter of notes we cannot name.
We can't begin again anywhere else

and since the only tradition is to err,
we live on memory & Bibb lettuce and

when life falls from sequence to drift-
wood, we linger, we legends of ruin.

PRECIPICE

It was a time most excellent—
before the turn, before the quick step
from our twin losses: *touch & yes.*

Before remembering, there was such time—
full smear of your honey-scent—
my coast of—our bout with stingless bees—

Every time that wasn't an absence was a plea.
Our colors (*fire and vanity*) held up.
Held close: one white peony

before metaphor became indispensable
in this least excellent time, this dawn
with no song—all wrens on vacation.

                    *

        Two apples, sliced,
        sit in a pool of twilight,
        in dreamscape, an agony
        of *never, already, too soon.*

LYNNE THOMPSON'S *Beg No Pardon* (Perugia Press, 2007) won
the Great Lakes Colleges New Writers' Award in 2008. Thompson was
commissioned to write poems for Scripps College's installation of a statue of
Harriet Tubman and for Emory University's choreographic staging of Warrior
Woman Pantoum. A Pushcart Prize nominee, her poems have been widely
published in literary journals including *Ploughshares, Sou'Wester, Indiana Review,*
Crab Orchard Review, among others, as well as the anthologies *New Poets of the*
American West and *Mischief, Caprice & Other Poetic Strategies*. Thompson is the
Reviews & Essays Editor of Tebot Bach's literary journal, *Spillway*.

CPSIA information can be obtained
at www.ICGtesting.com
Printed in the USA
FSOW03n0605190217
30850FS